MARTIN KETTLE
07901552168

THE TEACHING OF REALITY

THE TEACHING OF REALITY

Śrī Śaṅkara Ācārya's
Tattvopadeśa

Translated by
WARWICK JESSUP

SCHOOL OF ECONOMIC SCIENCE

This translation first published in 2014 by
The School of Economic Science
11 Mandeville Place, London W1U 3AJ
www.schooleconomicscience.org

ISBN: 978-0-9565968-5-7

The Sanskritpada™, SComp™ and Flags2™ Sanskrit fonts used in this book are designed and distributed by David Hockley, Oxford (tel. 01844 339944);
© 2003 David Hockley.

Cover: sculpture of Ādi Śaṅkara by Devalankunda Vadiraj
Photograph © Richard Wythe
Cover design by ml design
Typeset by Alacrity, Chesterfield, Sandford, Somerset
Printed and bound in the United Kingdom
by s|s|media limited, Rickmansworth, Hertfordshire

DEDICATED TO

HIS HOLINESS SHRI SHANTANANDA SARASWATI MAHARAJ JI

ACKNOWLEDGMENTS

The following should be acknowledged: Mr Leon MacLaren, for his initial inspiration in the study of *Advaita*, Dr Satyanarayana Sastry, the Rev. Dr Stephen Thompson, Mrs Isabelle Glover and Mr Paul Douglas for their helpful comments, Mr Michael Croza-Ross for typing the whole text and suggesting improvements, and Mr Donald Lambie for proposing the translation and providing constant support. Any errors are the responsibility of the translator.

INTRODUCTION

Tattvopadeśa, literally 'the pointing out' (*upadeśa*) of reality (*tattva*), is one of many works attributed to Ādi Śaṅkara, the first of the Śaṅkara Ācāryas, and the most eminent exponent of *Advaita Vedānta*. It is here rendered into English – to the best of our knowledge for the first time.

'*Vedānta*' means 'end of the Veda', referring to the Upaniṣads. The Upaniṣads occur at the end of each of the four Vedas, the compositions which are at the basis of the Sanskrit tradition. Literally, '*veda*' simply means 'knowledge'. So '*vedānta*' can be taken as 'the culmination of knowledge'.

'*Advaita*' means 'non-duality'. It is this non-duality which is taught by the sentence 'You are That' (*tat tvam asi*). This sentence is said to convey the essence of the entire teaching of the Upaniṣads. *Tattvopadeśa* offers insight into how 'You are That' (*tat tvam asi*) should be understood.

Words have layers of meanings, and to discover the true meaning of a word or sentence in its context, correct analysis needs to take place. In considering the great statement 'You are That' (*tat tvam asi*), the system of analysis adopted by the *Tattvopadeśa* is, in essence, elimination (*vyatireka*) followed by positive realisation (*anvaya*). Superimposed erroneous meanings of 'You' (*tvam*), such as being a body, and of 'That' (*tat*), such as omniscience, are eliminated, clearing the way for the positive realisation of the Absolute (*brahman*). The text explores the implied meaning (*lakṣaṇā*) within 'You are That' (*tat tvam asi*) and analyses how the sentence operates as a whole to bring about the realisation of non-duality (*advaita*).

It is clear that this analysis is not just an intellectual exercise but rather an essential part of the process of reflection, with its three aspects – hearing the words (*śravaṇa*), application of the mind (*manana*), and profound understanding (*nididhyāsana*). Besides this, the text emphasises the importance of having a teacher, in accordance with the statement 'One who has a teacher knows' (*ācāryavān puruṣo veda*), *Chāndogya Upaniṣad* 6:14:2. A number of versions of the Sanskrit text have been considered, and the most likely readings adopted.

THE TEACHING OF REALITY

तत्त्वम्पदार्थशुद्ध्यर्थं गुरुः शिष्यं वचोऽब्रवीत्।
वाक्ये तत्त्वमसीत्यत्र त्वम्पदार्थं विवेचय॥ १॥

1 The Teacher spoke these words to his disciple[1] in order to make clear the meaning of the word 'reality' (*tattva*). "Ponder[2] the significance of the word 'You' (*tvam*) in the sentence 'You are That' (*tat tvam asi*)."[3]

1 The word here for Teacher is *'guru'* and the word for disciple is *'śiṣya'*. The *guru-śiṣya* relationship is key in the Sanskrit tradition for the communication of knowledge. According to *Bhagavad Gītā*, chapter 4, verse 34, the seeker after knowledge needs to show reverence towards the teacher (*praṇipāta*), to fully pursue questions with the teacher (*paripraśna*) and to serve the teacher (*sevā*).

2 The advice given by the teacher begins here and continues for the remainder of the text. The word for 'ponder' is *'vivecaya'* from the root *'vic'* from which also comes the key term *'viveka'*, discrimination between the real and the unreal, the eternal and the transient.

3 One of the four great sentences of *advaita*, the teaching of non-duality, is *'tat tvam asi'* [You (*tvam*) are (*asi*) That (*tat*)] — see *Chāndogya Upaniṣad* 6:8:7 and subsequent sections. Since the verb 'to be' is often omitted in Sanskrit, this sentence could be abbreviated to *'tat tvam'*, and if these two words are written together, as they would be in a Sanskrit manuscript, they would appear as *'tattvam'*, the nominative singular form of *'tattva'*. Hence the great sentence *'tat tvam asi'* is a natural starting point for a treatise teaching about *'tattva'*, 'reality'.

न त्वं देहोऽसि दृश्यत्वादुपजात्यादिमत्त्वतः ।
भौतिकत्वादशुद्धत्वादनित्यत्वात्तथैव च ॥ २ ॥

2 You (*tvam*) are not the body, because it is an object of perception and is subject to birth and death etc.[4] Besides, it is a material substance which is impure and ever changing.

अदृश्यो रूपहीनस्त्वं जातिहीनोऽप्यभौतिकः ।
शुद्धनित्योऽसि दृग्रूपो घटो यद्वन्न दृग्भवेत् ॥ ३ ॥

3 You (*tvam*) are not an object of perception. You (*tvam*) are beyond form. You (*tvam*) are not subject to birth and death. Also, you (*tvam*) are devoid of material substances. You are pure and eternal, of the nature of an observer. A material substance like a pot could not be an observer.

4 The Sanskrit here simply says 'birth etc.', implying the various stages through which the body passes, such as birth, childhood, youth, old age and death. See also *Bhagavad Gītā* 2:13: "Just as the embodied one observes the stages of childhood, youth and old age in the body, so there is the taking on of another body; a wise person is not deluded in this matter" (*dehino'smin yathā dehe kaumāraṃ yauvanaṃ jarā; tathā dehāntaraprāptir dhīras tatra na muhyati*). Here the 'embodied one' is said to be the eternal Self.

न भवानिन्द्रियाण्येषां करणत्वेन या श्रुतिः ।
प्रेरकस्त्वं पृथक्तेभ्यो न कर्ता करणं भवेत् ॥ ४ ॥

4 You are not the senses,[5] for organs such as the ear are instruments. You are the origin, distinct from organs of sense. You could not be an agent or an instrument.

नानैतान्येकरूपस्त्वं भिन्नस्तेभ्यः कुतः शृणु ।
न चैकेन्द्रियरूपस्त्वं सर्वत्राहम्प्रतीतितः ॥ ५ ॥

5 Hear why you are distinct from the organs of sense. The senses are many, while you (*tvam*) are by nature one. Nor are you (*tvam*) of the nature of a single sense organ, for you know yourself in all circumstances as 'I' (*aham*).[6]

5 According to Manu, there are five senses of knowledge and five senses of action — all ten being presided over by mind (*manas*). [See the *Laws of Manu*, chapter 2, verses 90 to 92.]

6 *Aham* is the pure consciousness of 'I', as opposed to *ahaṅkāra*, which is *aham* associated with some *kāra* (activity).

न तेषां समुदायोऽसि तेषामन्यतमस्य च।
विनाशेऽप्यात्मधीस्तावदस्ति स्यान्नैवमन्यथा ॥ ६ ॥

6 You are not a combination of the senses, nor are you any particular sense organ. This must be true, for even when the senses disappear you are still aware of yourself.

प्रत्येकमपि तान्यात्मा नैव तत्र नयं शृणु।
नानास्वामिकदेहोऽयं नश्येद्भिन्नमताश्रयः ॥ ७ ॥

7 Listen! It is also unreasonable to think of yourself as the senses operating in sequence one by one, for this body, having various masters, would then perish, being reliant on divergent views.

नानात्माभिमतं नैव विरुद्धविषयत्वतः।
स्वाम्यैक्ये तु व्यवस्था स्यादेकपार्थिवदेशवत् ॥ ८ ॥

8 Neither can it be supposed that you are various selves, for they would have fields of action at variance with each other; but a master would be established as one, as in the case of a country with one king.

न मनस्त्वं न वा प्राणो जडत्वादेव चैतयोः ।
गतमन्यत्र मे चित्तमित्यन्यत्वानुभूतितः ॥ ९ ॥

9 You (*tvam*) are not the mind (*manas*), nor the vital force (*prāṇa*), for these are inanimate.[7] For we experience absent-mindedness in the form 'My mind was elsewhere'.

क्षुत्तृड्भ्यां पीडितः प्राणो ममायं चेति भेदतः ।
तयोर्द्रष्टा पृथक्ताभ्यां घटद्रष्टा घटाद्यथा ॥ १० ॥

10 We also experience separation from the vital force in the form 'This, my life, is oppressed by hunger and thirst'. The observer of these two is separate from them, just as the observer of a pot is separate from the pot.

7 Having established that the true Self is beyond the *annamayakośa* [the sheath (*kośa*) made up (*maya*) of food (*anna*)], namely the body, and also that It is beyond the senses which operate through the body, the text now seeks to establish that the Self is beyond the sheaths made up of the vital force (*prāṇamayakośa*) and mind (*manomayakośa*). In verse 11 the sheath of intellect (*vijñānamayakośa*) will be shown to be transcended, and finally in verse 12 it will be shown that the Self is distinct from the bliss sheath (*ānandamayakośa*) known in deep sleep.

सुप्तौ लीनास्ति या बोधे सर्वं व्याप्नोति देहकम्।
चिच्छायया च संबद्धा न सा बुद्धिर्भवान्द्विज ॥ ११ ॥

11 O twice-born, you are not the intellect (*buddhi*), which is bound by the shadow of consciousness (*cit*), which is dissolved in deep sleep, and which pervades the whole body when one is awake.

नानारूपवती बोधे सुप्तौ लीनातिचञ्चला।
यतो दृगेकरूपस्त्वं पृथक्तस्य प्रकाशकः ॥ १२ ॥

12 In the waking state the very unsteady intellect takes on manifold forms, and in deep sleep is absorbed. You (*tvam*) are the observer, by nature one, illuminating that from which you are distinct.

सुप्तौ देहाद्यभावेऽपि साक्षी तेषां भवान्यतः।
स्वानुभूतिस्वरूपत्वान्नान्यस्तस्यास्ति भासकः ॥ १३ ॥

13 Although the body etc. are absent in deep sleep, you are still the witness. Since by nature you experience yourself, you are not different from that which you cause to appear.

प्रमाणं बोधयन्तं तं बोधं मानेन ये जनाः ।
बुभुत्स्यन्ते त एधोभिर्दग्धुं वाञ्छन्ति पावकम् ॥ १४ ॥

14 Those people who wish to realise through thought (*māna*)[8] that consciousness which powers the means of knowledge (*pramāṇa*),[9] are like those who wish to use fuel to burn fire itself.[10]

विश्वमात्मानुभवति तेनासौ नानुभूयते ।
विश्वं प्रकाशयत्यात्मा तेनासौ न प्रकाश्यते ॥ १५ ॥

15 The Self (*ātman*) experiences the universe; the Self is not experienced by the universe. The Self illumines the universe; the Self is not illumined by the universe.

8 The word '*māna*', from the Sanskrit root for 'to think' (*man*), can imply the whole range of thought processes from opinion, notion, conception, idea, purpose, wish, design, to self-conceit, arrogance and pride.

9 The *pramāṇa* or 'means of knowledge', according to Vedānta, are six in number, namely sense perception (*pratyakṣa*), inference (*anumāna*), comparison (*upamāna*), revelation (*śabda*), non-perception (*anupalabdhi*) and inference from circumstances (*arthāpatti*).

10 Fire itself burns fuel, just as consciousness itself powers the means of knowledge. Fuel cannot burn fire itself just as thought and other means of knowledge cannot reveal consciousness itself.

ईदृशं तादृशं नैतन्न परोक्षं सदेव यत्।
तद्ब्रह्म त्वं न देहादिदृश्यरूपोऽसि सर्वदृक् ॥ १६ ॥

16 You are that Absolute (*brahman*), the observer of all, which is verily present and realiseable, but is not of a particular kind with a form of something visible such as a body.

इदम्त्वेनैव यद्भाति सर्वं तच्च निषिध्यते।
अवाच्यतत्त्वमनिदं न वेद्यं स्वप्रकाशतः ॥ १७ ॥

17 That which appears as this universe (*idam*) is being eliminated as well as all that which appears as 'That' (*tat*).[11] The reality (*tattva*) is not of this universe and cannot be expressed or known, since it is evident by itself.

11 This sentence anticipates the later analysis of 'You are That' (*tat tvam asi*), substituting 'this universe' (*idam*) for 'You' (*tvam*). See verses 40 and 41.

सत्यं ज्ञानमनन्तं च ब्रह्मलक्षणमुच्यते।
सत्यत्वाज्ज्ञानरूपत्वादनन्तत्वात्त्वमेव हि॥१८॥

18 It is said that the Absolute (*brahman*) is characterised as truth (*satya*), knowledge (*jñāna*) and infinity (*ananta*).[12] You are that Absolute (*brahman*), for you are full of truth, you are by nature knowledge, and you are infinite.

सति देहाद्युपाधौ स्याज्जीवस्तस्य नियामकः।
ईश्वरः शक्त्युपाधित्वाद्द्वयोर्बाधे स्वयम्प्रभः॥१९॥

19 When there are the limiting adjuncts (*upādhi*) of body etc., the personal soul (*jīva*) appears to limit the Absolute (*brahman*). This takes place when there is perception of duality as a result of the self-luminous Supreme Being (*īśvara*) appearing to be subject to the limiting adjuncts of its own powers (*śakti*).

12 This is a reference to *Taittirīya Upaniṣad* 2:1:1, 'The Absolute (*brahman*) is truth, knowledge and infinity' (*satyam jñānam anantam brahma*).

अपेक्ष्यतेऽखिलैर्मानैर्न यन्मानमपेक्षते।
वेदवाक्यं प्रमाणं तद्ब्रह्मात्मावगतौ मतम् ॥ २० ॥

20 The Absolute (*brahman*) is the source of all conceptions, but has no need of any conception. It is accessed through the sentences of the Veda, and known when one knows oneself (*ātman*).

अतो हि तत्त्वमस्यादिवेदवाक्यं प्रमाणतः।
ब्रह्मणोऽस्ति यया युक्त्या सास्माभिः सम्प्रकीर्त्यते॥ २१ ॥

21 Therefore we have proclaimed the Vedic sentences 'You are That' (*tat tvam asi*) etc. as the valid means of knowledge (*pramāṇa*) of that Absolute (*brahman*) through reasoning (*yukti*).

शोधिते त्वम्पदार्थे हि तत्त्वमस्यादि चिन्तितम्।
सम्भवेन्नान्यथा तस्माच्छोधनं कृतमादितः ॥ २२ ॥

22 When the meaning of the word 'You' (*tvam*) is made clear, 'You are That' (*tat tvam asi*) etc. is understood. There is no other way of achieving this than the purificatory process with which we began this treatise.[13]

देहेन्द्रियादिधर्मान्यः स्वात्मन्यारोपयन्मृषा।
कर्तृत्वाद्यभिमानी च वाच्यार्थस्त्वम्पदस्य सः ॥ २३ ॥

23 The directly expressed meaning (*vācyārtha*) of the word 'You' (*tvam*) is 'one who conceives of agency etc. and has falsely superimposed on the Self the characteristics of body, senses etc.'

13 See verses 2 to 21 inclusive, all of which have been clarifying the word 'You' (*tvam*).

देहेन्द्रियादिसाक्षी यस्तेभ्यो भाति विलक्षणः ।
स्वयं बोधस्वरूपत्वाल्लक्ष्यार्थस्त्वम्पदस्य सः ॥ २४ ॥

24 The indirectly expressed meaning (*lakṣyārtha*) of the word 'You' (*tvam*) is 'one who is the witness of the body, senses etc. who shines distinct from them, being by nature conscious by itself.'

वेदान्तवाक्यसम्वेद्यविश्वातीताक्षराद्वयम् ।
विशुद्धं यत्स्वसम्वेद्यं लक्ष्यार्थस्तत्पदस्य सः ॥ २५ ॥

25 The indirectly expressed meaning (*lakṣyārtha*) of the word 'That' (*tat*) is the pure imperishable non-duality beyond the universe, to be known through the statements of the Upaniṣads (*vedānta*), and to be discovered for oneself.

सामानाधिकरण्यं हि पदयोस्तत्त्वमोर्द्वयोः ।
सम्बन्धस्तेन वेदान्तैर्ब्रह्मैक्यं प्रतिपाद्यते ॥ २६ ॥

26 The two words 'That' (*tat*) and 'You' (*tvam*) agree with each other grammatically; through this agreement the Upaniṣads teach the unity of that Absolute (*brahman*).[14]

भिन्नप्रवृत्तिहेतुत्वे पदयोरेकवस्तुनि ।
वृत्तित्वं यत्तथैवैक्यं विभक्त्यन्तकयोस्तयोः ॥ २७ ॥

27 Though the two words are the cause of different manifestations, they refer to one reality (*vastu*), and so they have the same grammatical case (*vibhakti*) endings.

14 This verse makes it clear that the indirectly expressed meanings (*lakṣyārtha*) of both 'That' (*tat*) and 'You' (*tvam*) are one and the same (see verses 24 and 25). This is further developed in verse 27.

सामानाधिकरण्यं तत्सम्प्रदायिभिरीरितम् ।
तथा पदार्थयोरेव विशेषणविशेष्यता ॥ २८ ॥

28 This grammatical agreement has been uttered by those who hold the tradition; in this way it is clear that the two words stand in the relationship of adjective and noun.[15]

अयं सः सोऽयमितिवत्सम्बन्धो भवति द्वयोः ।
प्रत्यक्त्वं सद्वितीयत्वं परोक्षत्वं च पूर्णता ॥ २९ ॥

29 Expressions such as 'He is this' and 'This is he' show the relationship existing between two entities. When these entities are understood as individual (*pratyaktva*) there is duality, and when they are understood indirectly[16] there is the fulness of unity.[17]

15 Here it is said that the relationship between 'That' (*tat*) and 'You' (*tvam*) is one of adjective (*viśeṣaṇa*) and noun (*viśeṣya*). Verse 29 makes it clear that, in this context, 'That' (*tat*) can be taken as an adjective or noun, and 'You' (*tvam*) can also be taken as an adjective or noun. 'That' and 'You' would conventionally be thought of as pronouns, but the text here widens the grammatical interpretation.

16 The Sanskrit here is '*parokṣatvam*' — literally 'being out of sight, beyond the eye'. This sentence paves the way for going beyond the normally accepted meanings of 'You' (*tvam*) and 'That' (*tat*) as discussed in verses 30 to 41 inclusive.

17 The Sanskrit here is '*pūrṇatā*' — literally 'fulness'. In the *Bṛhadāraṇyaka Upaniṣad* 5:1:1, the word '*pūrṇa*' is used to describe the Absolute (*brahman*) according to the interpretation of Śrī Śaṅkara Ācārya.

परस्परविरुद्धं स्यात्ततो भवति लक्षणा।
लक्ष्यलक्षणसम्बन्धः पदार्थप्रत्यगात्मनोः ॥ ३० ॥

30 'That' (*tat*) and 'You' (*tvam*) could be seen as mutually incompatible; therefore their implied meaning (*lakṣaṇā*)[18] is understood. There is a close connection between what is being implied — namely the inner Self (*pratyagātman*) — and the implied meaning of the words.

मानान्तरोपरोधाच्च मुख्यार्थस्यापरिग्रहे।
मुख्यार्थस्याविनाभूते प्रवृत्तिर्लक्षणोच्यते ॥ ३१ ॥

31 If the normally accepted (*mukhya*) meaning of a word leads to inconsistency with other information, then — without completely discarding the normally accepted meaning — an implied meaning (*lakṣaṇā*) is said to apply.[19]

18 *Lakṣaṇā* is from the root *lakṣ*, 'to indicate'.

19 Compare with verse 47 of *Vākyavṛtti*, a similar work attributed to Śrī Śaṅkara Ācārya.

त्रिविधा लक्षणा ज्ञेया जहत्यजहती तथा।
अन्योभयात्मिका ज्ञेया तत्राद्या नैव सम्भवेत् ॥ ३२ ॥

32 It should be known that there are three types of implied meaning: the first, in which the directly expressed meaning is discarded; the second, in which the directly expressed meaning is not completely discarded; and the third, in which both of these apply.[20] In the case of 'You are That', the first type is certainly not relevant.[21]

20 To clarify the implied meanings of *tat* and *tvam*, the text here enumerates the three types of implied meaning (*lakṣaṇā*):

(a) ***jahatī lakṣaṇā 'the implied meaning discarding (the directly expressed meaning)'*** — This is when the directly expressed meaning (*vācyārtha*) is discarded. A stock Sanskrit example is 'a hamlet on the Ganges', which actually means 'a hamlet on the bank of the Ganges'. The directly expressed meaning 'on the Ganges' is discarded. Otherwise the hamlet would be waterlogged!

(b) ***ajahatī lakṣaṇā 'the implied meaning not discarding (the directly expressed meaning)'*** — This is when the directly expressed meaning (*vācyārtha*) is not completely discarded, and a word indicates the meaning of another word previously used, as in the stock Sanskrit example 'This red runs', meaning 'This red horse runs', referring to a reddish bay horse. The directly expressed meaning of 'red' is not discarded, for it refers to something that is red. However, the sense of another word ('horse') previously used is implied by the word 'red'.

(c) ***jahatī-ajahatī lakṣaṇā 'the implied meaning both discarding and not discarding (the directly expressed meaning)'*** — This is when one part of the directly expressed meaning (*vācyārtha*) of a statement is discarded and another part is not discarded. In the case of 'You are That' (*tat tvam asi*), temporal features are discarded and the eternal is not discarded. A stock Sanskrit example is 'He is this sage', in which, in the context of a continuous passage, 'he' refers to what is not immediately evident but was

वाच्यार्थमखिलं त्यक्त्वा वृत्तिः स्याद्या तदन्विते।
गङ्गायां घोष इतिवज्जहती लक्षणा हि सा॥ ३३ ॥

33 When the directly expressed meaning is completely discarded, the meaning in the context can be clear, as in 'A hamlet on the Ganges', where 'on the Ganges' is taken in the context to mean 'on the bank of the Ganges'. This is the first type of implied meaning.

वाच्यार्थस्यैकदेशस्य प्रकृते त्याग इष्यते।
जहती सम्भवेन्नैव सम्प्रदायविरोधत॥ ३४ ॥

34 When the directly expressed meaning is only discarded in one respect, this is not regarded as the first type of implied meaning, as this would not be in keeping with the tradition (*sampradāya*).[22]

Continued from previous page:
previously seen, and 'this' refers to what is present. When these temporal features of past and present are discarded, one is just left with 'sage', to which both 'he' and 'this' refer. The implied meaning of 'sage' is not discarded. In the same way, with 'You are That' (*tat tvam asi*) the mutually incompatible implied temporal features of '*tat*' and '*tvam*' are discarded, and the mutually compatible implied meaning of 'eternal Absolute' is not discarded (see note on verse 41).

21 It is not the case that the directly expressed meaning of 'You are That' (*tat tvam asi*) is simply discarded. Traditionally the third type of implied meaning is used to elucidate this great sentence.

22 The tradition regards this second type of implied meaning, spoken of in verses 34 and 35, as inadequate for the realisation of 'You are That' (*tat tvam asi*). '*Virodhata*' does not make good sense, so here is translated as '*virodhataḥ*'.

वाच्यार्थमपरित्यज्य वृत्तिरन्यार्थके तु या।
कथितेयमजहती शोणोऽयं धावतीतिवत् ॥ ३५ ॥

35 When the directly expressed meaning is not discarded, and a word is used in the sense of another word previously used, this is regarded as the second type of implied meaning as in 'This red runs', 'red' referring to a red horse.

न सम्भवति साप्यत्र वाच्यार्थेऽतिविरोधतः।
विरोधांशपरित्यागो दृश्यते प्रकृते यतः ॥ ३६ ॥

36 Here also the meaning is not that of the directly expressed meaning, for that would not make sense; the expression is partially meaningful in that 'red' does apply to a horse being implied.

वाच्यार्थस्यैकदेशं च परित्यज्यैकदेशकम्।
या बोधयति सा ज्ञेया तृतीया भागलक्षणा ॥ ३७ ॥

37 When in one way the directly expressed meaning is not present, and in another it is present, then that is the third type of implied meaning.

सोऽयं विप्र इदं वाक्यं बोधयत्यादितस्तथा।
तत्कालत्वविशिष्टं च तथैतत्कालसम्युतम् ॥ ३८ ॥

38 The sentence 'He is this, a sage' sheds light on this. 'He' has been previously identified and 'this' indicates someone present.

अतस्तयोर्विरुद्धं तत्तत्कालत्वादिधर्मकम्।
त्यक्त्वा वाक्यं यथा विप्रपिण्डं बोधयतीरितम् ॥ ३९ ॥

39 Therefore, when the features of any particular time etc. which are opposed to each other are abandoned, the sentence points out the body of the sage.

तथैव प्रकृते तत्त्वमसीत्यत्र श्रुतौ शृणु।
प्रत्यक्त्वादीन्परित्यज्य जीवधर्मांस्त्वमःपदात् ॥ ४० ॥

40 Now that all this has been put forward, hear 'You are That' as spoken in the revealed teaching (*śruti*), completely discarding[23] from the word 'You' (*tvam*) the qualities of the soul (*jīva*) such as being inner (*pratyak*).

23 Here even the notion of the Self being inner is given up, completing elimination (*vyatireka*) of part of the directly expressed meaning (*vācyārtha*) of the word 'You' (*tvam*) [see verse 23]. This clears the way for positive realisation (*anvaya*).

सर्वज्ञत्वपरोक्षादीन्परित्यज्य ततःपदात् ।
शुद्धं कूटस्थमद्वैतं बोधयत्यादरात्परम् ॥ ४१ ॥

41 When from the word 'That' (*tat*) omniscience or imperceptibility etc. are completely discarded,[24] with attention the supreme, pure, unchanging non-duality (*advaita*) is awakened.

तत्त्वमोः पदयोरैक्यमेव तत्त्वमसीत्यलम् ।
इत्थमैक्यावबोधेन सम्यग्ज्ञानं दृढं नयैः ॥ ४२ ॥

42 From the two words 'That' (*tat*) and 'You' (*tvam*) unity is realised. The sentence 'You are That' is sufficient for this. Thus, through the awareness of unity, the wise firmly establish true knowledge.

24 To guard against importing notions about the Absolute, here even the notions of omniscience or imperceptibility etc., pertaining to the Absolute as the creator, are given up. Verses 6 and 7 of the *Māṇḍūkya Upaniṣad* also distinguish between the omniscient creator (*prājña*) and the non-dual Absolute (*turīya*) respectively. Śaṅkara on verse 6 comments: 'Since this one is the knower in all states of diversity, he is omniscient.' By discarding notions of omniscience etc. there is elimination (*vyatireka*) of part of the directly expressed meaning (*vācyārtha*) of the word 'That' (*tat*). Now that the incompatible directly expressed meanings of 'You' (*tvam*) and 'That' (*tat*) are discarded, the directly expressed meaning which is now realised to be present in both, namely the Absolute, is positively realised (*anvaya*). This is *jahatī-ajahatī-lakṣaṇā*, applicable to both 'You' and 'That'. 'Are' (*asi*) implies the identity of these two terms. This marks an evolution of understanding as compared to verses 24 and 25, in which it is said that only the

अहं ब्रह्मेति विज्ञानं यस्य शोकं तरत्यसौ।
आत्मा प्रकाशमानोऽपि महावाक्यैस्तथैकता॥ ४३॥

43 One who knows in experience that 'I am Absolute (*brahman*)'[25] transcends grief. The Self (*ātman*) becomes evident through the great statements (*mahāvākya*).[26] In this way there is oneness.

तत्त्वमोर्बोध्यतेऽथापि पौर्वापर्यानुसारतः।
तथापि शक्यते नैव श्रीगुरोः करुणां विना॥ ४४॥

44 Or, the awareness of the Self is awakened by 'That' (*tat*) and 'You' (*tvam*) in succession. Nevertheless, this is not possible without the compassion of a blessed teacher.[27]

Continued from previous page:
indirectly expressed meanings of 'You' (*tvam*) and 'That' (*tat*) reveal the Absolute. This direct realisation is later referred to – for example in verse 48 – by such phrases as '*pratyakṣāt parijñātam*' (literally 'fully known in front of the eyes').

25 'I am Absolute' (*aham brahmāsmi*) is another great statement (*mahāvākya*). See *Bṛhadāraṇyaka Upaniṣad* 1:4:10.

26 The other two great statements (*mahāvākya*) are 'This Self is Absolute' (*ayam ātmā brahma*) [*Bṛhadāraṇyaka Upaniṣad* 4:4:5] and 'Knowledge is Absolute' (*prajñānaṃ brahma*) [*Aitareya Upaniṣad* 5:3], making four in all.

27 In the remainder of *Tattvopadeśa* the importance of a teacher is often emphasised. See verses 46, 47, 75, 78 and 84 to 87.

अपरोक्षयितुं लोके मूढैः पण्डितमानिभिः ।
अन्तःकरणसंशुद्धौ स्वयं ज्ञानं प्रकाशते ॥ ४५ ॥

45 In the world those who are deluded only feign wisdom. But when they cultivate purity of the mind (*antaḥkaraṇa*) to realise the presence of the Self, knowledge spontaneously shines forth.

वेदवाक्यैरतः किं स्याद्गुरुणेति न साम्प्रतम् ।
आचार्यवान्पुरुषो हि वेदेत्येवं श्रुतिर्जगौ ॥ ४६ ॥

46 With these statements from the Veda, one may think there is no need for a teacher. Such a position is incorrect, for the revealed teaching (*śruti*) has asserted that one who has a teacher knows.[28]

अनादाविह संसारे बोधको गुरुरेव हि ।
अतो ब्रह्मात्मवस्त्वैक्यं ज्ञात्वा दृश्यमसत्तया ॥ ४७ ॥

47 For here, in this beginningless round of birth and death (*saṃsāra*), it is the teacher who causes one to know. In this way, realising the unity of the Absolute (*brahman*) and oneself (*ātman*), one knows the visible as insubstantial.

28 See *Chāndogya Upaniṣad* 6:14:2, 'One who has a teacher knows' (*ācāryavān puruṣo veda*).

अद्वैते ब्रह्मणि स्थेयं प्रत्यग्ब्रह्मात्मना सदा।
तत्प्रत्यक्षात्परिज्ञातमद्वैतब्रह्मचिद्घनम् ॥ ४८ ॥

48 Remain ever in the non-dual Absolute (*brahman*), through the inner Self which is the Absolute (*brahman*). That being fully known in reality, there is the wealth of consciousness which is that non-dual Absolute (*brahman*).

प्रतिपाद्यं तदेवात्र वेदान्तैर्न द्वयं जडम्।
सुखरूपं चिदद्वैतं दुःखरूपमसज्जडम् ॥ ४९ ॥

49 The Upaniṣads elucidate that very Absolute (*brahman*) but not the inert world of duality. This non-dual consciousness is by nature bliss, while the inert, which is unreal, is by nature misery.

वेदान्तैस्तद्द्वयं सम्यङ्निर्णीतं वस्तुतो नयात्।
अद्वैतमेव सत्यं त्वं विद्धि द्वैतमसत्सदा॥ ५० ॥

50 The Upaniṣads completely distinguish duality from true wisdom. Know that non-duality (*advaita*) alone is true and that duality is ever unreal.

शुद्धे कथमशुद्धः स्याद्दृश्यं मायामयं ततः।
शुक्तौ रूप्यं मृषा यद्वत्तथा विश्वं परात्मनि॥ ५१॥

51 How can there be impurity in purity? Therefore the perceptible is illusory (*māyā*). Just as one erroneously perceives silver in an oyster shell, so one erroneously perceives the universe in the supreme Self.[29]

विद्यते न स्वतः सत्त्वं नासतः सत्त्वमस्ति वा।
बाध्यत्वान्नैव सद्द्वैतं नासत्प्रत्यक्षभानतः॥ ५२॥

52 Nothing exists independently. Nor does anything come from that which does not exist. Therefore duality does not exist, yet it appears to exist.

सदसन्न विरुद्धत्वादतोऽनिर्वाच्यमेव तत्।
यः पूर्वमेक एवासीत्सृष्ट्वा पश्चादिदं जगत्॥ ५३॥

53 That which exists is not non-existent, for that would be contradictory. Therefore that which was at first one alone and then, having created, became this universe, cannot be explained in any way.

29 Nacre or mother-of-pearl is an iridescent substance found inside oyster shells. It can be mistaken for silver.

प्रविष्टो जीवरूपेण स एवात्मा भवान्परः।
सच्चिदानन्द एव त्वं विस्मृत्यात्मतया परम् ॥ ५४ ॥

54 You are that same supreme Self (*āṭman*) which has entered into the form of an individual soul (*jīva*). You are being (*sat*), consciousness (*cit*) and bliss (*ānanda*) and nothing else.[30] Yet you forget your supreme Self (*ātman*).

जीवभावमनुप्राप्तः स एवात्मासि बोधतः।
अद्वयानन्दचिन्मात्रः शुद्धः साम्राज्यमागतः ॥ ५५ ॥

55 Though having taken on the form of an individual soul (*jīva*), at the dawn of true knowledge there is the realisation that you are that very Self, which is pure and is simply non-dual bliss and consciousness. You are the universal sovereign.

कर्तृत्वादीनि यान्यासंस्त्वयि ब्रह्माद्वये परे।
तानीदानीं विचार्य त्वं किंस्वरूपाणि वस्तुतः ॥ ५६ ॥

56 Now that you — the supreme non-dual Absolute (*brahman*) — have examined such notions as being the doer (*kartṛ*), which used to inhere in you, the question arises 'What is your true nature?'

30 *'eva'* is here translated as 'and nothing else'.

अत्रैव श्रृणु वृत्तान्तमपूर्वं श्रुतिभाषितम् ।
कश्चिद्गान्धारदेशीयो महारत्नविभूषितः ॥ ५७ ॥

57 Right now hear the unprecedented tidings of the revealed scripture (*śruti*): There was a man from the region of Gāndhāra[31] who was adorned with large jewels.

स्वगृहे स्वाङ्गणे सुप्तः प्रमत्तः सन्कदाचन ।
रात्रौ चौरः समागत्य भूषणानां प्रलोभितः ॥ ५८ ॥

58 On one occasion, intoxicated, he fell asleep in the yard of his own house. At night thieves came, lured by the jewels.

31 See *Chāndogya Upaniṣad* 6:14:1 for this story. Gāndhāra was the name given to a region which is now partly in Afghanistan and partly in Pakistan. In the epic *Mahābhārata*, Gāndhārī is a princess who came from this area. She was betrothed to King Dhṛtarāṣṭra, and on discovering that he was blind, she blindfolded herself for almost the whole of the rest of her life. The great grammarian Pāṇini is also said to have come from this region.

बद्ध्वा देशान्तरं चौरैर्नीतः सङ्गहने वने।
भूषणान्यपहृत्यापि बद्धाक्षकरपादकः ॥ ५९ ॥

59 The thieves took him off to another country, and brought him to a dense forest. They snatched the jewels, blindfolded him, and tied up his hands and feet.

निक्षिप्तो विपिनेऽतीव कुशकण्टकवृश्चिकैः।
व्यालव्याघ्रादिभिश्चैव सङ्कुले तरुसङ्कटे ॥ ६० ॥

60 He was thrown down into a thicket teeming with trees, sharp blades of grass, thorns, scorpions, and with beasts of prey such as tigers.

व्यालादिदुष्टसत्त्वेभ्यो महारण्ये भयातुरः।
शिलाकण्टकदर्भाद्यैर्देहस्य प्रतिकूलकैः ॥ ६१ ॥

61 He was distressed by the hostile beasts in that great forest, and the rocks, thorns and sharp blades of grass that were making his body so uncomfortable.

क्रियमाणे विलुठने विशीर्णाङ्गोऽसमर्थकः ।
क्षुत्तृडातपवाय्वग्न्यादिभिस्तप्तोऽतितापकैः ॥ ६२ ॥

62 During the robbery his limbs had been broken and now he was incapacitated, severely afflicted by hunger, thirst, by the biting ice-cold wind and then by the blistering heat of the sun.

बन्धमुक्तौ तथा देशप्राप्तावेव सुदुःखधीः ।
ददृशे कञ्चिदाक्रोशन्नैकं तत्रैव तस्थिवान् ॥ ६३ ॥

63 He had lost hope of being freed from his bonds, let alone of returning to his own country. He remained there crying out for help, but saw no-one.

तथा रागादिभिर्वर्गैः शत्रुभिर्दुःखदायिभिः ।
चौरैर्देहाभिमानाद्यैः स्वानन्दधनहारिभिः ॥ ६४ ॥

64 In the same way, the multitude of attachments — such as thinking of yourself as the body — are enemies causing misery and are thieves stealing away the wealth of your own bliss.

ब्रह्मानन्दे प्रमत्तः स्वाज्ञाननिद्रावशीकृतः ।
बद्धस्त्वं बन्धनैर्भोगतृष्णाज्वरादिभिर्दृढम् ॥ ६५ ॥

65 Though in the bliss of the Absolute (*brahman*), you became intoxicated, overcome by the sleep of your own ignorance (*ajñāna*). You are bound fast by fetters such as feverish thirst for pleasure (*bhoga*).

अद्वयानन्दरूपात्त्वां प्रच्याव्यातीव धूर्तकैः ।
दूरनीतोऽसि देहेषु संसारारण्यभूमिषु ॥ ६६ ॥

66 These extremely deceptive forces divert you from your nature (*rūpa*), which is non-dual bliss (*ānanda*). You are then led far away into bodies grounded in the forest of transmigration (*saṃsāra*).

सर्वदुःखनिदानेषु शरीरादित्रयेषु च।
नानायोनिषु कर्मान्धवासनानिर्मितासु च॥ ६७॥

67 In various births, fashioned by the latent impressions (*vāsanā*) of those blinded by action (*karma*), you find yourself amidst triads such as body, mind and heart,[32] which are the cause of all miseries.

प्रवेशितोऽस्मि सृष्टोऽस्मि बद्धः स्वानन्ददृष्टितः।
अनादिकालमारभ्य दुःखं चानुभवन्सदा॥ ६८॥

68 You are introduced into the womb[33] and created, prevented from experiencing your own bliss, but rather ever experiencing misery (*duḥkha*) from time without beginning.

32 The creation is regarded as triformal, as for example in the *Māṇḍūkya Upaniṣad*, which speaks of the waking, dreaming and deep sleep states, corresponding to the body, mind and heart, or the physical, subtle and causal worlds.

33 See also *Śrīmad Bhāgavatam* (Skandha 3, chapter 31) in which the sage Kapila first describes how the ignorant individual soul (*jīva*) enters the womb, and then vividly depicts the miseries of being in the womb.

जन्ममृत्युजरादोषनरकादिपरम्पराम् ।
निरन्तरं विषण्णोऽनुभवन्नत्यन्तशोकवान् ॥ ६९ ॥

69 Full of grief and despondency, you continually experience a succession of such hells as the detrimental effects of birth, old age and death.

अविद्याभूतबन्धस्य निवृत्तौ दुःखदस्य च ।
स्वरूपानन्दसम्प्राप्तौ सत्योपायं न लब्धवान् ॥ ७० ॥

70 You have not found the way of truth, in which the misery of the bondage of ignorance ceases and in which the bliss that is your own nature is regained.

यथा गान्धारदेशीयश्चिरं दैवाद्दयालुभिः ।
कैश्चित्पान्थैः परिप्राप्तैर्मुक्तदृष्ट्यादिबन्धनः ॥ ७१ ॥

71 As with the man from the region of Gāndhāra, after a while, he who is excluded from the teaching of liberation etc. is, by good fortune, found by some travellers who take pity on him.

सः स्वस्थैरुपदिष्टश्च पण्डितो निश्चितात्मकः ।
ग्रामाद्ग्रामान्तरं गच्छेन्मेधावी मार्गतत्परः ॥ ७२ ॥

72 Those healthy souls direct him to a wise man (*paṇḍita*) of firm conviction. He, now endued with wisdom, and intent on finding the way, would go from village to village.

गत्वा गान्धारदेशं स स्वगृहं प्राप्य पूर्ववत् ।
बान्धवैः सम्परिष्वक्तः सुखी भूत्वा स्थितोऽभवत् ॥ ७३ ॥

73 He, arriving in the region of Gāndhāra, again came home, was embraced by his relations, and was happy.

त्वमप्येवमनेकेषु दुःखदायिषु जन्मसु ।
भ्रान्तो दैवाच्छुभे मार्गे जातश्रद्धः सुकर्मकृत् ॥ ७४ ॥

74 You also in this way have wandered perplexed through many births which confer misery. By good fortune, performing good deeds, with your faith aroused, you have set off on an auspicious path.

वर्णाश्रमाचारपरोऽवाप्तपुण्यमहोदयः ।
ईश्वरानुग्रहाल्लब्धो ब्रह्मविद्गुरुसत्तमः ॥ ७५ ॥

75 The best of teachers is the knower of the Absolute (*brahman*). That teacher who is attentive to the proper response in each situation,[34] and has attained the auspicious final liberation, is found through the grace of the Supreme Being (*īśvara*).

विधिवत्कृतसन्न्यासो विवेकादियुतः सुधीः ।
प्राप्तो ब्रह्मोपदेशोऽद्य वैराग्याभ्यासतः परम् ॥ ७६ ॥

76 Following the practice of non-attachment, a wise person who is endued with discrimination and who has, in accordance with the scriptures,[35] given up all claims, now accepts the teaching regarding the Absolute (*brahman*).

34 It is said here that the best of teachers is attentive to the conduct appropriate to each function in society (*varṇa*) and stage of life (*āsrama*). This conduct is seen in the Sanskrit tradition as summing up the whole field of right action (*dharma*).

35 *'vidhivat'* is here translated as 'in accordance with the scriptures'. *'Vidhi'* is an injunction from the *Veda*. The implication is that life is led inspired by the directions given in the revealed teaching of the *Veda* (*śruti*).

पण्डितस्तत्र मेधावी युक्त्या वस्तु विचारयन्।
निदिध्यासनसम्पन्नः प्राप्तो हि त्वं परं पदम्॥ ७७॥

77 You are such a learned wise person, discriminating the real from the unreal. Having come to profound understanding (*nididhyāsana*),[36] you have assuredly realised the Supreme.

अतो ब्रह्मात्मविज्ञानमुपदिष्टं यथाविधि।
मयाचार्येण ते धीर सम्यक्तत्र प्रयत्नवान्॥ ७८॥

78 Therefore I, acting as teacher, have, in keeping with the scriptures,[37] pointed out to you, O wise one, who have made proper efforts on this path, the knowledge (*vijñāna*) of that Absolute (*brahman*) which is your Self (*ātman*).

36 *'nididhyāsana'*: Reflection on statements from the revealed teaching (*śruti*) is said to have three stages — hearing the words (*śravaṇa*), application of mind (*manana*), and profound understanding (*nididhyāsana*). See *Bṛhadāraṇyaka Upaniṣad* 4:5:6.

37 *'yathāvidhi'* is here translated as 'in keeping with the scriptures'. It is stated that the teaching has taken place through and in harmony with the revealed teaching of the *Veda* (*śruti*).

भूत्वा विमुक्तबन्धस्त्वं छिन्नद्वैतात्मसंशयः ।
निर्द्वन्द्वो निःस्पृहो भूत्वा विचरस्व यथासुखम् ॥ ७९ ॥

79 Released from bondage, with doubts about the unity of the Self cut asunder, devoid of duality and desire, act freely.

वस्तुतो निष्प्रपञ्चोऽसि नित्यमुक्तः स्वभावतः ।
न ते बन्धविमोक्षौ स्तः कल्पितौ तौ यतस्त्वयि ॥ ८० ॥

80 In reality you are beyond proliferation (*prapañca*), ever free by nature, never subject to bondage or liberation, for these are only imagined by you.

न निरोधो न चोत्पत्तिर्न बद्धो न च साधकः ।
न मुमुक्षुर्न वै मुक्त इत्येषा परमार्थता ॥ ८१ ॥

81 You do not die, nor were you born. You are not bound, nor are you an aspirant. You are not one desirous of liberation, nor are you one who is liberated. This is the highest Truth.[38]

38 Verse 81 is quoting *Māṇḍūkya Kārikā* 2:32.

श्रुतिसिद्धान्तसारोऽयं तथैव त्वं स्वया धिया।
सम्विचार्य निदिध्यास्य निजानन्दात्मकं परम् ॥ ८२ ॥

82 This is the essence of the revealed teaching (*śruti*),which you have discovered through your own intelligence and through the profound realisation that you are the Supreme (*para*), which is innately blissful.

साक्षात्कृत्वा परिच्छिन्नाद्वैतब्रह्माक्षरं स्वयम्।
जीवन्नेव विनिर्मुक्तो विश्रान्तः शान्तिमाश्रय ॥ ८३ ॥

83 Being directly aware of the detached non-dual indestructible Absolute (*brahman*) Itself, completely free and at ease, rest in stillness while yet living.

विचारणीया वेदान्ता वन्दनीयो गुरुः सदा।
गुरूणां वचनं पथ्यं दर्शनं सेवनं नृणाम् ॥ ८४ ॥

84 The Upaniṣads should be reflected upon, and the teacher always venerated. The words of teachers are salutary; human beings benefit from seeing teachers and serving them.

गुरुर्ब्रह्म स्वयं साक्षात्सेव्यो वन्द्यो मुमुक्षुभिः ।
नोद्वेजनीय एवायं कृतज्ञेन विवेकिना ॥ ८५ ॥

85 The teacher is the Absolute (*brahman*) Itself right in front of your eyes. The teacher should be served and shown honour by those desirous of liberation, and should certainly not be feared by one who is discriminating and of right conduct.

यावदायुस्त्वया वन्द्यो वेदान्तो गुरुरीश्वरः ।
मनसा कर्मणा वाचा श्रुतिरेवैष निश्चयः ॥ ८६ ॥

86 For as long as you live the Upaniṣads should be venerated, and the teacher should be venerated as the Lord. This is the resolution: that the revealed teaching (*śruti*) alone should live in mind, action and speech.

भावाद्वैतं सदा कुर्यात्क्रियाद्वैतं न कर्हिचित्।
अद्वैतं त्रिषु लोकेषु नाद्वैतं गुरुणा सह ॥ ८७ ॥

87 One should always cultivate the feeling of non-duality[39] (*advaita*), but never impose non-duality (*advaita*) on the field of practical dealings (*kriyā*). One should cultivate non-duality (*advaita*) in all three worlds, physical, subtle and causal,[40] but one should not cultivate non-duality (*advaita*) with the teacher.[41]

39 Literally 'one should always make non-duality (*advaita*) by/from/of/in feeling (*bhāva*).' This word *bhāva* is very wide-ranging, and can be taken as being, existing, state, condition, truth, reality, manner of being, nature, temperament, character, manner of acting, conduct, any state of mind or body, way of thinking or feeling, sentiment, opinion, disposition, intention, meaning, passion, emotion, love, affection, attachment, that which is or exists, a thing or substance.

40 See note 32 on verse 67 regarding the triformal view of creation. In the present verse *kuryāt* ('one should make'), here translated as 'one should cultivate/impose', could be supplied in the second, third and fourth quarters of the verse, or these quarters could be taken as statements of fact, namely that there is no non-duality (*advaita*) in action, there is non-duality (*advaita*) in the three worlds, but no non-duality (*advaita*) with the teacher.

41 The teaching of non-duality (*advaita*) proposes two levels of reality, namely ultimate reality (*paramārtha*) and the field of practical dealings (*vyavahāra*), here referred to simply as 'action' (*kriyā*). Teacher and pupil are one aspect of the field of practical dealings, so one should not impose non-duality (*advaita*) on this relationship. The text has already stated in verse 86 that for as long as one lives the teacher should be venerated as the Lord.